2021 A.D.

An Illustrated Short Story of
My Journey Through an Illusion of the World

2021 A.D.
An Illustrated Short Story of
My Journey Through an Illusion of the World

Eric Manning

2021 A.D.
An Illustrated Short Story of
My Journey Through an Illusion of the World

Table of Contents

Preface 1

Chapter 1: "Tree of Fear" 3

Chapter 2: "Childhood Coffin Shack".............................6

Chapter 3: "Dead Butterflies . . . Come to Life" 8

Chapter: 4 "Bloody Butterflies" 10

Chapter 5: "My Dreaded Future" 11

Chapter 6: "A Grieving and Weeping" 13

Chapter 7: "A Wicked Branch"..15

Chapter 8: "Wicked Clench"...17

Chapter 9: "A Blazing Fire"..19

Chapter 10: "A. Rat Bastard" 21

Chapter 11: "Voices Behind the Tree" 24

Chapter 12: "The Rat Bastard Speaks Clearly" 27

Chapter 13: "Out of the Darkness" 29

Chapter 14: "A Welcoming"..31

Chapter 15: "A Fruitful Tree"...32

Chapter 16: "The Search for Water" 34

Chapter 17: "Faces of Adoration" 36

Chapter 18: "A Battle Going On"....................................39

Chapter 19: "Spiral Haze . . . In a Daze"........................41

Chapter 20: "Falling Apart"...44

Chapter 21: "A New Face"...47

Preface

Thistons piece started with inspiration from a song called, "Dead Butterflies" by Architects. After listening to the lyrics, they moved me so deeply because I related it to the death of my own childhood and how deeply disturbing that has been for me, even now, in adulthood. Which is why I named this piece "2021 A.D." with a tombstone as an icon denoting this meaning. As I related the lyrics with my own story, I began to sketch a coffin with butterflies coming out of it. While I sketched, I continued to remember

the many different relationships and events in my childhood that led to the death of it. This is the reason for the left side of the piece being so dark and dreary. But for me, I also experienced another side which surprisingly woke my soul from the dead. This is shown in the top center and top right sections with the coffin representing my childhood being in limbo between spiritual life and death.

I envisioned a "tree of fear" that represents all the horrifying experiences of my childhood, that became so deeply rooted that it was never possible for me to escape. Whenever I reflect upon that horrid tree of fear, I realize just how deep the roots go into my heart and soul. The roots from that fearful tree continued to affect my teenage years and then followed me all the way into adulthood. At times, I did anything possible to escape the hellish roots of my past which always had a very intense spiritual, psychological, emotional, and even physical effect on me throughout my life. It was like my heart being "torn out" by a branch of this wicked tree that has controlled much of my life and has kept me a prisoner within it.

The faces on the tree represent and express many of the terrible and broken relationships I have experienced with my parents, grandparents, relatives, teachers, school peers, coaches, neighborhood friends, and many others. The bitter roots of the tree connected all the dark and broken experiences I had with others around me, which came from the same sinister place. The blood drips from my wounded heart, as it is gripped by one of the branches, and spatters on the ground. This would happen after each time my parents had a vicious fight. In the end, one of them would usually blame me for it, and then I could hear the voice of the wicked tree inside me say, "You are a bad child and I hate that you even exist!"

When I reflected on these horrifying times in my life, I saw that these words came from the many deadly wounds I received as a child. I remember how I could never let go of any of them or forget them for very long. At certain moments as a child and teenager, I did learn how to cope with them, and suppress these unwanted thoughts and feelings, and had even gotten good at it as I grew into adulthood. To cope or "numb" myself psychologically and emotionally, I had to embrace particular things of the world around me that did not involve interacting with people and, quite often, I ended up isolating myself.

Eventually, I realized my wounds would never heal. The grip of fear on my heart from the branch on the tree was just too strong and it would never let me go no matter how much time would pass. All I could see within the relationships I experienced in my house was the end of my life on earth with no hope in sight. Destruction and despair were rooted inside my heart, and death was all around me.

"What have I done or said that was so wrong to be accused and hated by my own family and so many others around me?" I would ask myself this so many times as a child, adolescent, and even later as an adult. For years, whenever I searched out in the world, I never got any answers to questions like this one. Somehow, at times, I could sense something very wrong deep inside my soul. But there was nothing I could do to stop this hellacious struggle within me.

My inner child had been stuck inside the darkness of what I pictured as a "coffin shack" for so long that I wanted to take a risk and see if there was something better outside of it. One day, "the child inside me" decided to peek out of the darkness, through a hole in my coffin shack, to respond to a light that was shining through it.

From very early on, my "inner child" took on an identity of who I truly believed I was, which seemed to come from the experiences I had with my parents. Desperate for freedom from the pain and isolation, I wanted to find out if there was any way out of the coffin shack. I wanted to know if there was anything good outside of the darkness inside my coffin shack, which became my own little world. It was full of resentment and hatred for myself and my family.

One day, through the small hole in the coffin shack, my inner child could see and feel water trickle down gently from a mysterious unknown source of light that I had amazingly experienced from above. Curious, yet leery, my inner child pushed up on the coffin shack lid and put a little pressure on it with his hand, and heard a board crack, snap, and break off. Just after the breaking of the board, the light above suddenly became much brighter through the hole he was peeking through, and it startled and blinded him just for a moment.

For my inner child experienced pain inside the darkness and despair of his coffin shack most all his life on earth. As a result of this, he was very afraid when the light above him illuminated the inside of his coffin with a strange and foreign compassionate expression of love.

After my "child inside" experienced bright-light illuminations inside the coffin shack a number of times, he started to communicate more clearly to my adult self and said, "Hey, what do we have to lose, there's nothing but darkness, death, and despair in this coffin shack!" After hearing his voice, I started to become

familiar with my inner child, who I had been so isolated from for so long. Being reacquainted with my inner child was miraculous to me. Much like a part of my heart and soul (which I had never known), had been raised from the dead!

Right after the miraculous occurrence of being reconnected with my child, I somehow mustered up the courage to take a risk and see if I can get him out of the darkness and despair he was in for so long. With his fingertips, I noticed, my inner child started to slowly slide the top of the coffin shack over a little, and then he noticed dead butterflies coming to life which lit up the inside of the coffin. In awe, we watched them come to life and begin to fly up and out of the cold and dark casket!

As I witnessed the events unfolding around my inner child, the colors on the butterfly's wings were very peculiar, and I noticed them dripping bright red blood from the top of their wings and it flowed down from their bodies. All around the butterflies, there was a yellow and orange fire blazing, with a white undertone. At about this same time, I noticed the coffin board (which he broke off from pushing on it) began to float higher above us and upward into the unknown source of light which was shining down brighter than ever.

The next unusual and beautiful vision that was revealed to me was a lotus flower blooming out from under the mud of a pond. Suddenly, I realized there was water drizzling from the pond and it was

splashing on my coffin shack. This vision continued and I saw something even stranger than ever before. The dirt, mud, and muck, floating under the pond, fell further than my eyes could even see.

Then I noticed a vibrant green grass growing upward and around the sides of the pond. I had to ask myself some questions, "Is this experience real or surreal? Where is it coming from? Am I perceiving these strange events on the inside of me or am I receiving some kind of 'out of body' spiritual experience that I've heard of other people having?" There was now something completely different, spiritual, and mystical going on inside and outside of my little dark and dreary world which changed my perspective of myself and others.

While trying to understand what was real or surreal, I turned my head and looked down beneath my coffin and saw a large tombstone that was cracked and had a big hole in the middle of it. The tombstone was engraved: "2021 A.D." and there was

blood dripping down from the letters. I knew right then and there this message was meant for me to notice and to heed in this moment. The experience was very difficult and was just like grieving at my own funeral. Finally, I broke down and started to weep over the loss of my life . . . from my broken and lost childhood all the way to now.

After this morbid and grievous experience, I paused in this dark and sobering moment. I reflected on all the horrible events and happenings of past broken relationships which led to my body and soul breaking down. It had become obvious that I had been holding onto a very sad, distorted, and broken identity of self which I could not escape no matter how hard I tried.

While focusing on the 2021 A.D. tombstone vision again, for just a moment, I began to experience an extremely painful and sick feeling within my stomach. What came to mind afterwards was the reality of the wounds inside me, which would eventually become fatal, and they were taking me into "the pit of hell," with no hope in sight to ever recover. The many broken and lost relationships (or friendships) that I had hoped would be reconciled one day, were not, and were never going to be. This led to unbearable, endless, and hopeless despair about them all.

Now, I had finally come to realize that the relationships with my parents, relatives, and so many others I had known, some for just a moment in time, were never going to be made right. I thought many times throughout my life, "Why was there always something wrong going wrong inside me?" Now, I finally understood why that was so. All the bad relationships inside my family as child, adolescent, and adult, progressed to desperation and sorrow. Because I could never let go of my broken heart, I knew I could never hold onto any kind of relationship, and I began to weep like never before.

As I was crying over my broken and lost life and relationships, I noticed there were many other human souls with faces on the smaller headstones around my larger "2021 A.D." tombstone. Many of the headstones came to life for a moment and expressed themselves with faces of disappointment and loss with an eternal sadness upon them. Although I could barely stand to look at the faces on the headstones, I could not turn away from staring at them in amazement. The headstones began grieving and weeping out loud saying, "My childhood, my life, my friendships, my relationships are lost forever! Can someone please help me find them?"

While I was still in the middle of my own unbearable grieving and weeping, I began to receive a mysterious consolation from the pain what was lodged deep within my gut. The unknown mystical being above me embraced me with a peaceful consolation that made the unbearable pain inside disappear instantly. Amazed in a supernatural awe, it seemed like I was now inside the presence of the being above me that I never knew existed. This was bizarre to me, and my mind could not understand why someone who experienced that they are so unworthy and unwanted, like myself, could have ever received such a loving embrace from someone who seemed so kind and loving.

Alittle later, after pondering the surprise spiritual experience I just had from up above, I noticed my child peeked back down out of his coffin at the world below. A wicked branch became animated out of the tree of fear and started shouting at and slandering the weeping souls who were expressing sadness out of their graves. The wicked branch shouted out, "Shut the hell up, nobody gives a damn about your lost childhood or relationships! Eventually, every child's soul in this God-forsaken place is lost and there is no hope inside this world of darkness, you fools!"

Another wicked tree branch, next to the slandering one, joined in with him, and let out a sarcastic cackle and said, "Yeah, what the hell are you thinking? No rest for the wicked in this lifetime!" The second wicked branch, who was laughing at and mocking the desperate souls of the animated headstones, then showed me my wounded heart that he had in his grip, and raised it up high and said, "Oh, you think you can be rescued from your bad experiences you had in your family since the day of your birth? Hahaha! You're a reject, you're damaged goods!"

15

"Think about that reality inside you again! Look at how many times you've tried to escape the hell you've lived in all your life, but you never could! Just stop and think for a minute about the impossibility of you ever changing your life into something good in this sad and pathetic life of yours! You have no chance in hell of escaping your past here! Besides, you were given no meaning or value by your parents, grandparents, relatives, neighbors, classmates, or anyone else in your pathetic little world, so why the hell would you ever entertain the belief that anyone else would, including the spirit of light from above?"

After hearing the horrible slander and discouragement coming from a branch of the tree of fear, I saw and felt the grip of my heart in the tree branch's fingers. The branch from the tree who held my heart in his grip, was keeping me trapped in a sort of trance within a desperate and hopeless state of mind. Then, I felt the wicked branch's grip on my heart get even tighter, and the pain multiplied, and I became even more desperate to escape it.

It was right after this dreadful experience, which felt like eternal hell for a moment, that I finally realized that I was powerless to escape from it by myself and had been living in this horrible reality all my life. All my attempts to break free from the wicked branch and tree of fear were futile. The tree seemed to possess me within my dark and dreaded past, with a deception and spirit which was unknown, but familiar at the same time.

My focus had then shifted away from the experience with the tree of fear and its wicked branches. I just could not help but take another cold hard look down below my casket once again. Only this time, there was a blazing fire burning underneath with a white-hot flame mixed with red, orange, and yellow colors. Fearful enough as the fire below me already was, the ground then began to shake and crumble under me. The grass, soil, and rocks underneath my coffin shack were coming loose and crumbling, falling into the endless white-hot flames and they were disintegrating right before my eyes.

Shortly after watching the ground fall apart underneath me, and disappear into the endless flames, I experienced another gut-wrenching pain mixed with fear and anxiety that felt like it was deep inside my stomach. The suffering I experienced felt both eternal and hopeless at the same time and I became more fearful than ever. Just after I thought it could not get any worse, it did.

After experiencing an intense amount of pain and suffering for a moment longer, I was finally brought to a place of humility and then I began to notice a desire to surrender the pain that came from deep within my mind, body, and soul. Not knowing if he would hear my call, I took a chance and cried out to the unknown spirit above me to see if he could somehow hear or respond to my desperate cry.

Then, after waiting for a response from the unknown spirit above, I had another moment of reflection and wondered how my life could have come to this most desperate and terrifying place still lingering deep within. "How could I be so full of guilt, shame, and dismay so early on in my life?" I sensed there was a very intense spiritual battle going on inside me in this moment, in the middle of all the intense confusion and dismay I was experiencing, which seemed like it was never going to end.

Somehow, I was led to make a humble and sober choice to expose the truth of everything that was going wrong inside and around me. With what little and feeble strength that I had in the moment, I asked the unknown spirit above me for help. Yes, crazy as it seemed to me, I asked the mysterious spirit above to rescue me from the direction that my life seemed to be going.

At this point, I knew, by my own efforts, there was no escape from my great distress and sorrow. I called out to the unknown and invisible spirit, "Can you help me escape from this sad truth I'm living in? It seems to me that it will be inevitable for me to fall deeper into the same darkness, pain, and isolation if you do not help, so please do! I now realize that my own heart and soul will lead me further away from anything good which I have experienced with you!"

Right after my desperate, and much needed, attempt to reach out to the unknown spirit-being above, it was suddenly revealed to me that "a dirty rat bastard" had set me up for this kind of fall long ago. My mind was illuminated with an understanding of a cold and hard truth of why I was presently in a dark and dreary state of being that was always getting worse. Humbling as this cold and hard truth was, it dawned on me that I could have never escaped or recovered from the relational wounds I experienced in my childhood home; for they were permanent. Permanent as the day, back in my early childhood, when I realized that I existed on the earth as a human.

The first thing I experienced, and identified with, was resentment and hatred. Violence, abuse, hopelessness, shame, and sorrow followed wherever I went. Even when my parents were not around me, it seemed as if an unknown dark and mysterious being was often speaking to my soul. At the end of each day, when I isolated myself, this dark spirit would tell me that it was my own bad self that made everything go wrong in my life. The dark spirit would not leave me alone and continued to blame me when things went wrong in life, both inside and outside my home. Whenever my parents' violent fights and unresolved issues came up and out inside the home, I was to blame for it and, each time it happened, my wounds got more severe.

The voice of the mysterious dark spirit that had been blaming me all the time, was finally revealed when the light from the kind spirit above shined his light upon me and spoke the truth to me deep within my heart. The light from above revealed that the dark spirit of many accusations was just a "dirty rat bastard." The "dirty rat bastard" was brought out from under the cellar of my soul and into the light by the spirit of compassion and love, and now I could see clearly what was haunting me. The "dirty rat bastard" had been behind all my troubles in life, the whole time!

Never could I have understood the reality that a "dirty rat bastard" spirit truly existed and affected my life without receiving a revelation from this kind unknown spirit-being up above me. The invisible but present "rat bastard" spirit consistently led me to believe that I was always the sole cause for my parents' marital failures and many breakdowns. With each day that passed, the "dirty rat bastard" would draw me into a family martyr role which reinforced the blame, and it grew into shame to the point of hopelessness and despair.

The blame and shame martyr role became an identity which progressed so deeply inside my mind, body, and soul, that it almost seemed normal for me to live in it every day. Whenever I had enough of my martyr role and reacted to it by running away from my home, I would always end up isolated and confused . . . . and deep in a forest near my house. Although my guilt and shame "martyr role" seemed to be normal in my relationships with my parents and relatives, it became normal with outsiders as well.

Fortunately, I never stopped seeking an answer to the question of why I was so downcast and miserable and that I could never really accept being blamed anymore. Eventually, I ended up hating myself for playing the role of the family martyr and then hating my parents for putting me in that role and then denying that they did. I was trapped.

For days, months, and even years, I asked myself, "Why do my parents contradict themselves with what they say and what they do? Why do they both despise the sight of me one day, and the next day tell me they love me? Why do my parents take turns reinforcing a guilt/shame complex within me using cruel and abusive tactics on a regular basis, and why can't they ever stop? Why do my grandparents resent and despise me more every time I am forced to visit them, and they never bother to listen to me or talk to me at all? Am I just a hopeless case, where my whole life crumbles down around me before I even reach my teenage years and young adulthood? Am I just an 'evil little bastard child' who deserves everything that happens to me because I have no good inside me at all? Am I destined to go down such a dark and painful path to my destruction or is there an escape to live another way?"

Although I pondered the direction of my life, heading towards death so often, this time I perceived it to be different and more eerie than ever. Now, along with my vision of a "dirty rat bastard" and a fresh understanding of the presence of fear in my life, I

could hear voices. Not audible voices like you hear from people, but voices that speak to your heart on a deeper level. But at the same time, I began to clearly process the language with my mind, seeing through all the intense pain and confusion that came from the role I was forced to play.

I now understood that the foul voices had a source: the tree of fear! With nothing but evil and discouraging words, which had been mocking and harassing me for years, I could now see and hear the tree of fear clearly speak to me, "Why do you even attempt to think of resolving your martyr role, and relational issues within your family, that you can never truly understand or do anything about? You attempt to cry out to some unknown 'good' spirit or deity up above for help in the present moment, but nobody was ever there for you since the day you were born, were they?"

"Now, just take a good hard look at what has happened to all your relationships thus far, and how they played out in your life. Most of them, including the ones with your father and mother, are badly twisted and damaged beyond any hope of reconciliation! Look at your relationships with your grandparents, relatives, and so-called friends. It's always the same cold hard truth! Lies, resentment, anger, and bitterness have taken over their hearts and souls and does that ever change? Hell no!"

"Now child, do you really believe that you can deal with this kind of twisted drama and distorted reality, which is inside you, too? Haha . . . . That amuses me! If some unknown spiritual being or 'God' above you really does have any care, compassion, or concern for you, then why are you so damn confused in your miserable life? Did you know that, right here and now, in the place you're living, most everyone that knows you at all views you as damaged goods or a bad kid?"

"Now child, think about it once again, does that sound like a good spiritual being or 'God' up above who created you, cares for you, or ever wanted to help you with your 'bad self or relationship issues? Maybe, if you just stop being concerned with what's wrong with you or your parents, life would not be so bad for you. Maybe if you stopped being so concerned about your relationships gone bad, especially your parents and relatives, you would not have to struggle so hard in this life and things would go better for you out in the world!"

After hearing the discouraging voice coming from behind the tree of fear, I was tempted to be apathetic and just not care or hope about changing for the better. The voice from the tree of fear seemed too strong and was very convincing in getting me to just accept my relationships, life, and myself for the downcast and hopeless soul which I was. In all the confusion, discouragement, and dismay that I had already experienced out in the world, I still thought about the other voice from above, which gave me transcendent peace and understanding.

Despite the convincing voice of the rat bastard, which seemed to be the same one coming from the tree of fear, I still knew I would never be okay and nothing in my life would be resolved and go in the right direction. The worst part about the voice coming from the dirty rat and the tree of fear, was that it never revealed who he or she was to me. I just knew something was wrong and could not understand why this was so.

After my mysterious experience with the unknown being up above, I knew that I wanted to hear something different than all the hate, confusion, and apathetic and discouraging words which were spoken to me by my parents, relatives, and others around me most of my life.

Now I knew from experience, that I had received something better from up above, and even though the message came and went so fast, the presence of it seemed to make a lasting impression. Something happened inside me that was good, from someone who I perceived to be real. A spiritual-being that was beyond all the turmoil of lies and numerous terrible relationships. The great amount of confusion in my life, which led me down to a hopeless and desperate state, was beginning to change for the better.

After many days of searching out in the world for someone who had similar spiritual experiences, I fell into many more bad situations and dark days, which were very distressing and discouraging. Fortunately, out of the many dark and long days searching for true friends, understanding, meaning, and purpose in my life, I finally again heard the call of the unknown mysterious being from above. He went into my heart and soul, and I was reunited with him.

Still, I was frightened and leery by his great presence because I really did not know what to think about, or how to respond to, the spirit who was obviously calling me to himself in a very peculiar way. The experiences that I had with the spirit above me were very impactful and intense, but in a good and peaceful way that was very different and difficult to comprehend.

After thinking about my experiences, I received a deeper revelation of who the spirit was and how he saw me. I began to ask myself the question, "Could this be the God that people on the earth seek inside of religion?" He seems so different than the god that so many attempt to represent inside of ministries I've attended but they always end up accusing me (and many others) of bad behavior and moral failures.

I waited for the answer to come to me for months and, finally, the strangely ironic, but peaceable presence of the spirit above came to me. This time he came as a compassionate, fiery, and eternal spirit that burned inside me.

His words then spoke a language to my heart, soul, and body which was so different from most of those I had been so accustomed to my whole life. It was hard to believe that all my experiences with his spirit and kind friendship (without any accusations) were even real.

The words the spirit spoke to me were gentle yet powerful, humble yet convicting. This dynamic spirit brought an awakening and renewal to me from somewhere deep inside my heart to a place my soul and body had never been. The spirit-being invited, welcomed, and accepted me in a way that I had been longing for all my life.

This eternal spirit's voice was so different than the voice I was much more familiar with from the tree of fear. In just a small moment in time, his spirit communicated a peace, calmness, kindness, and friendship inside me, in a way that no one on earth had ever done. After so many years of being manipulated and lied to, the spirit-being transcended that with a timeless message of healing and deliverance to my body, mind, and

soul. This took me all the way back to where I was so deeply wounded.

The whole spiritual experience I just received was quite a miracle of hope in the present moment, and the timing seemed perfect. In the past, I experienced the roots of fear, hatred, and shame so many times that they became deeply entangled within me. I believed they were permanent. Worst of all, I was always very afraid of dying and remaining in my dark and hopeless state (resented and unloved forever), but now that had finally changed.

After my unexpected and mysterious revelation with the unknown spirit-being from above, I began to see a whole new perspective of my life from the inside out. My view of the world around me began to change as well. I gained a perspective of life that I never knew existed. It gave me some freedom from the dark and shameful past of toxic family relationships that I was never able to confront alone. At first, the new perspective was difficult to understand and adjust to because I was not used to relating to God or other people with such freedom. I was used to being manipulated and so, to protect myself from harm, I was very guarded.

Eventually, I understood that my soul had been awakened by just a moment of authentic compassion, forgiveness, acceptance, friendship, and love by a powerful spirit who cared. Now, I was more liberated than ever to enjoy the forests I used to run to for shelter whenever fighting broke out in my home and my family's hatred and accusations landed on me. Magically, the forests, trees, rivers, and streams around me now seemed like they were there for me to enjoy without having thoughts and feelings of guilt or shame.

Now, I could see a friendly face behind all the nature around me through the great spirit above. In the past, I was reluctant to trust or believe anyone or anything that was good for me. I was now able to receive and enjoy things without fearing there was a price to pay. This time it was different. In the past, if I was allowed to enjoy something in life, someone (e.g. my parents) always had an ulterior motive. So, I ended up resenting anyone being kind, understanding, or giving. I did not trust that they freely gave to me out of the kindness of their heart. But now, quite the contrary turned out to be true.

This was a new reality in my world. The mysterious spirit was without any "strings" or conditional motives attached to him. Somehow, I was now able to look beyond the darkness to see an eternal light behind of all the colors of nature shining from above and through all the different trees of the forest. There was a beautiful rest and peace I was now receiving from a greater love and altruistic spirit when I was alone in the forest.

There was an odd fruitful tree I now envisioned, and it had a constant flow of water coming from its mouth and had patches of grass growing around it. The tree also had ponds near the grass that flowed into its roots, which were not connected to the earth's soil, but from the spirit's world above. Scratching my head, I wondered why the fruitful tree's root source and soil were separated and were not planted on the soil of the earth. Was the mysterious spirit from up above making the fruitful tree grow all by himself? Why was he showing me this separation in a vision inside my mind? What was he trying to communicate to me? Why was I now experiencing such a deep longing to be in his presence, which transcended all the darkness of the past that hurt me so much?

Maybe, I thought, this was another true and authentic spiritual experience without any strings attached (i.e. lies, hatred, or abuse). Again, I looked back up at the tree that was drizzling water down near me, and I put my mouth underneath it and was able to drink from it for the first time. After I could drink no more, I felt at peace and at rest and was more satisfied than ever before. I noticed that I had no fear of guilt, shame, or manipulation inside me at all in this blissful moment. Then, I heard a voice from the spirit above that mysteriously spoke to my soul again, "You can drink as much as you want without any cost. Keep on drinking from my water source, it will make you well in a way you cannot imagine at this time in your life."

After I was done drinking for a while, I looked back up and noticed that the fruitful tree had faces of adoration looking up into the light source above them. They were all singing in harmony together up into the light of the spirit above them that had gotten so bright that I could not make out a face, body, or image behind it. After having experienced the spirit from above a few different times now, I could not help myself, but to think about how I did not deserve it, earn it, or work for it. Somehow, I was able to just simply believe and receive the spirit's care and love without condition.

Now, I wondered how I could ever continue to live in the presence of this loving and kind spirit from above. His light was so bright, and the world that I was used to was so dark and dreary, that I could not even bear to look up to see who or what he was. Many more questions now came to my mind from deep within my heart. Now I could envision a stark dichotomy between good and evil inside me and it felt very unnerving at times. How, I thought, was I ever going to be able to make the right choices in the present day to walk away from the old ways of living?

This seemed impossible again and I was fearful whenever I thought about it. Most of my life, I knew I made many bad decisions where I was never able to control their consequences. Even when I did not want them to, my choices usually ended with me feeling fearful, shameful, and hateful towards myself and defensive towards most people I knew. Yeah sure, I did have a few enthralling moments throughout my life, but in the world I knew, most were fleeting, and I could never hold onto them for long. In the end, the choices I made had always led me to being isolated, lonely, and depressed in my relationships with others, but most of all with my parents.

Most of the time, my life was about surviving the relationships at home with my resentful and hateful parents, my grandparents, other relatives, and authority figures in or outside of public school. For the longest time, I wondered why I just had to settle for, and to cope with, the pain and dismay that I experienced throughout most days of my life. I also wondered why I had so little hope of ever getting better or going in the right direction with my life, and I had no idea who I was inside myself or what I ever wanted to be.

Although many people around me seemed to have more self-esteem and confidence than I did most times, I eventually realized that some of them were trying to cope with their lives just like I was. It was clear to me that some were better at coping with or dealing with challenging tasks and problematic issues in their lives than others were. I could never quite understand why this was so.

The most difficult and confusing situations often came when I tried to communicate my questions and perceptions about life and relationships. It was incredibly difficult when I asked others about these types of relational questions and then why things would somehow go wrong inside of them. "Why," I pondered for so long, "was there such a ferocious battle going on inside me over all of these unanswered questions?"

The biggest resistance always came when I asked anyone questions about why my parents' relationship was so terrifying, hateful, and seemed to be "going to hell in a handbasket." So, I finally asked the big question to the spirit above, "Why did I have to go on a ride of horror inside my parents' relationship? I never chose them for parents in the first place and I always hoped that they would divorce to stop their fighting and throwing accusing curses at me."

Chapter 18: "A Battle Going On"

It seemed whenever I tried to speak out and express myself from the heart about what I experienced inside of me, there was a resistance of some kind. Usually, I was either verbally or physically attacked or ignored completely. My parents would become defensive, angry, and violent when I expressed the truth of how or why they are acting and relating to each other and myself.

Eventually, I gave up trying to have an honest, truthful conversation with my parents because it became obvious that they had no intention of having one with me. From a very young age, I had no other choice but to go outside of my home to search for someone, anyone out in

the world, who I could truly communicate with to find deeper understanding. I found no one.

By the time I was around eleven to twelve years old, there were times when I could communicate, or relate on a deeper level, with other kids around my age. Although, for some unknown reason, conversations would seem to stop before we ever got to the heart of the matter. The problem was when I continued a conversation, and attempted to get bluntly honest with my peers, there were few to none who seemed to understand or care enough about what was going on inside me or themselves.

Some people would respond to me in fear by saying, "Oh, that's too deep" or "Yeah don't go there and open that can of worms!" Other people would ignore me completely or quickly dismiss what I had to say about my personal issues that came from the heart. They would say, "I don't want to even think about that kind of thing, it's too much for me," and then change the subject to something more superficial.

I was shut down and rejected by so many people that I met outside my home (in my school or out in the streets somewhere). Despite this, I still tried my best to communicate with anyone out in the world who was

willing to go a little deeper in conversation. Eventually, after many attempts to communicate with people outside my home, I gave up trying and kept my mouth shut and just listened to others talk.

I hated feeling so isolated and alone and trapped inside my dark and dreary world without being able to express it. Longing and desperately needing acceptance from people, I would try to forget all my troubles with the best of what the world had to offer me at the time. Many times, when out in the streets, I did whatever I could to stay the hell away from my childhood home. The best that I thought that I could ever do was to keep my eyes open for someone out there to connect with.

The problem was, I was always looking over my shoulder in fear of what would happen if I did communicate what was truly inside me. Never being sure of what was happening inside me most of the time, and what reaction I would get when talking about it to those around me, I knew had to be careful and I was very cautious of being hurt and rejected again. Constantly, I wondered in confusion about why the relationship with my parents was so bad, with no hope in sight. And why were the friendships outside my home either shallow or falling apart to the point where I had to leave them and search somewhere else? Eventually, I thought that I might be the cause for all my friendships going wrong, as my parents and grandparents said I was, and many others around me indicated I was.

The question of fault did come up for me in my conscience many times during my childhood and teen years and even young adulthood. Many authorities in public school and church accused me of being rebellious against their authority. Was it the nature of my outlandish, crazy, and bad behavior towards others that was bringing me down to the pit of hell? When I was outside my home, and I got too deep into "soul searching" for these answers, I noticed that I often would be captivated by things in the world, which would help me escape from the dark reality I lived in daily.

There were things offered to me in the world, such as drugs and alcohol, and the arts and music culture, which I loved very much. They became very spiritual for me. In my mind's eye, I pictured the "spirit of the world" much like a spiral haze that could be hypnotic, deep within my soul. Whenever I was out and about in the world and relating to people "on the level" which was acceptable to many of my friends, most of them seemed to have an ugly self-centered agenda lurking behind them.

There was always a hopelessness at the end of all of these "hypnotic" experiences. After a while, they haunted my soul with that hopelessness and now, even more unresolved relational issues. Eventually, I did learn how to cope with my unresolved issues, questions about myself, and others around me. It felt good and there was a sense of freedom in it. Through the thrills and fleeting pleasures of the world I took part in, I learned how to numb my pain and bury my sorrows. Nonetheless, the relational issues deep inside continued to haunt me and I was never really in control of any of them.

The more common or "typical" conversations I had with those in my neighborhood, or kids that I went to school with, did give me a little more consolation and hope that things might get better at times. The needed relief from reality I received was always temporary. My attempts to communicate and develop friendships with others seldom lasted. After this harsh reality set in, my default reaction was to go back to a particular spiritual state of being, which I perceived to be odd or "spiritually hazy" from drugs, music, and the arts.

At other times in my life, I could escape the pain through playing the joker, which worked if, and only if, I could make people laugh. The painful and unfortunate events that I experienced (and the relationships with my parents) were unbearable so I had to find an outlet for the pain. The trick of playing the clown was to indirectly make fun of my dysfunctional family issues in front of others. When I did, it gave me much needed relief.

The problem was that the tragic comedy I created, and all the laughter afterwards, just helped me cope with my distress in the moment. No matter how amusing I became to my peers, my comedic outlet never really changed the horrifying family relationships I had no choice but to endure. I knew I was still unraveling inside. The hilarious good times kept coming but never lasted long enough for me to escape the dark reality within; they did not last long enough to obtain any real or long-lasting friendships or trust with anyone. At the end of my jokes, I knew nothing was really all that funny about my life or how it all played out. In the end, I would always fall apart psychologically, emotionally, and even physically sometimes, and had to isolate myself from my family and everyone else for long periods of time.

Eventually, after each day's distress and isolation, I knew I had to go back home. And when I did, I never knew when I would, once again, get blamed, shamed, and eventually attacked and hurt by my parents. When I was forced to go on trips upstate to visit my grandparents (who also resented me) this would just pile on more blame. My role was always to play the scapegoat. My parents never had any intention of being accountable for their violent and hurtful actions. They never would work out their personal issues, which were destroying their own lives, along with mine. After a while, it was obvious that they were never going to change, no matter how many times they attended church, how much marital counseling they got, or how many religious seminars they went to over the years.

The anticipation of going back home again and having to look at my father's face of resentment and rejection, and my mother's vicious accusations, led to an intense fear and loathing I could never escape. The fear of this darkness inside me would dominate most of my life until I finally moved far away from my parents for good.

One evening, about a year later, I was even deeper into the roots of fear and darkness of my wicked past. A very shocking new face was finally revealed. It seemed ironic how the face of the unknown spirit above me came to illuminate my soul in my darkest hour. Out in the world, and all alone for the first time in my life, I experienced the horrifying reality of what was truly going on inside me. Without any distractions or interference from the broken relationships with my parents and the familiar environment where I grew up, I began to see the deep wounds inside me that I had attempted to cover up for over two decades.

The pain and wounds from the past did not go away after leaving home and traveling many miles across the United

States. The wounds were just too deep within me to handle on my own, and it was obvious to me that I was going to eventually self-destruct without some kind of miraculous help. As much as I tried to self-medicate, the pain and wounds of the past broken relationships with my parents, grandparents, and many others haunted me in the present day more intensely than ever before.

Although I did my very best to distract myself from the pain inside by taking college classes, working, exercising, listening to music, and partying with drugs and alcohol, I just could not leave the past behind. The pain and suffering inside my soul in the present, began to scare the hell out of me a little more each day that I tried to cover them up. I successfully escaped from my hometown, which reduced the pain of the broken relationship with my parents. Nonetheless, the bitter roots and wounds of my childhood, which were still in my heart, followed me seventeen hundred miles west and I realized they were with me to stay.

After many days and long nights, I realized that I was helpless and hopeless to change myself from the inside-out. The spiritual being (who I now thought could possibly be the real God) once again surprised me out of nowhere and revealed His love, compassion, and kindness to me. His Spirit did this in a way that surpassed all the horror I was experiencing all alone and without any distractions or comfort from anyone around me.

Finally, I realized the Spirit-being, which I was now more familiar with, was the source of the water flow I envisioned, and from Him was bright light illuminating it. In my lonely and very vulnerable state at the time, far from home, the impact of this spiritual experience was undeniable and was very ironic because of the image of God that was projected by religion in my childhood.

The way I experienced God through my parents and other leaders in organized religion wounded me deeply. So, the deity of God and Son, taught by religious judgmental leadership, disgusted me, and turned me off from ever wanting to believe or have anything to do with Him.

Despite the disgust from my past, a new face of compassion and love surprised the hell right out of me. In the deepest and darkest depths of my wounded heart and soul, I had no idea that His Spirit could or would transcend my entire dark and broken past. From my perspective, it seemed as though I made too many bad choices in the past for me to receive anything good from anyone, much less compassion and love from an unknown God who truly existed and personally interacted with me.

Honestly, I hated organized religion and church services with a passion, and I thought that would have disqualified me (after so many religious people said it would) from knowing or understanding anything good from God and His Son. It turned out that all those past religious experiences, which attempted to control my behavior, were just false pretenses and a lie from the pit of hell.

The many horrifying religious experiences of judgment and condemnation that I had with my parents, grandmother, some relatives, and even my so-called "friends" led me astray from the reality and irony of the true spirituality I now experienced with God.

Unfortunately, most of the people I knew from my hometown had related to me in a personal and spiritual way contrary to what I found to be true in God's nature. Yes, it was quite the unorthodox miracle that I experienced with a spiritual and unconditional acceptance from God and Son without any religious rituals or interference from religious leaders.

A new face was revealed to me that was not accusing, rejecting, judging, or condemning based on what I did right or wrong in the past or how I tried to cope with my "bad self" in the present. God's Spirit was concerned with what was going on inside my heart and not so much with how I expressed it on the outside. It was revealed to me that all God was calling me to, was to face the truth about the state I was in, and then trust Him one baby-step at a time. It was then that I began to authentically surrender my personal issues to Him, instead of trying to hide them. These issues had haunted me my whole life in my relationships from childhood to the present day.

Both surprisingly and miraculously, here I am today in 2021 A.D., writing a story about another painting I envisioned over two decades after I started my spiritual journey. Still, I am seeking guidance and inspiration from God and Son. And still, I'm taking it one step at a time and humbly learning how to let go of my past painful and wounded relationships. As a result, I can receive a new relationship of compassion, love and friendship and have a greater peace with Him and others in the present.